I0467277

A Tax Guide 4 Foreigners:

Investing, Working or Living in the United States

MARY VIGAL, J.D., LL.M. (Tax)

ISBN-13: 978-1499175790

ISBN-10: 1499175795

Dedication

To the Condado Group LLC, which operates with a global mission to timely educate and assist foreigners and their advisors on U.S. tax issues and strategies. www.condado-group.com

CONDADO GROUP

TABLE OF CONTENTS

INTRODUCTION:

A foreign person is classified for U.S. income tax purposes by the Internal Revenue Service, the "IRS", as either a resident alien, green card holder or a nonresident alien; and for estate and gift tax purposes, as either a domiciled or a non-domiciled foreigner. Each of these classifications can have very different tax results for the foreigner. So many different terms with such different tax results! How is a foreign person to understand all of this and make the right choices? Immigration definitions for a foreigner's status in the U.S. are not the same as the tax definitions

A U.S. corporation is one that is incorporated under the laws of one of the 50 States or the District of Columbia. The place of incorporation is what is important. A foreign corporation is one that is not formed under the laws of one of the States or the District of Columbia. Unlike the U.S., in many countries, the management and control of a corporation can determine where a foreign company is deemed to be resident.

This booklet provides an introduction to the U.S. income and transfer tax system and how to maneuver through the rules successfully. It discusses the tax consequences for foreigners when investing in U.S. real estate and the tax planning opportunities available. Often a foreigner is not ready for the U.S. tax system and risks penalties for failure to report and file on time. The wish to operate in a tax effective manner is answered in this simple to read guide.

PART ONE: INCOME TAXES

1. Foreign persons who spend time in the U.S.: Resident Aliens and Green Card Holders

A resident alien or green card holder is subject to federal income tax on worldwide income. The income tax treatment is the same as for U.S. citizens.

If a foreigner is determined to be a resident of the U.S., and also in another country, generally some relief is available if there is an income tax treaty between the U.S. and the other country.

Green Card Test:

The first test for income tax residency in the U.S. is the "green card test."

This is a person who, for immigration purposes, has been admitted to the U.S. as a permanent resident and has received a green card. Once a foreign person acquires a green card and holds it for eight years or more, they cannot leave the U.S. tax system without having to comply with the expatriation rules.

Substantial Presence Test:

A second test is the "substantial presence test".

The substantial presence test is a far more difficult test then the green card test to determine residency status. Too many days visiting in the U.S. can make a foreigner an accidental income tax resident! The test is tricky because there are several ways to count physical presence.

Residency under this test begins on the first day of physical presence in the U.S. for the year that residency begins. Residency terminates on the last day of the calendar year in which a foreigner qualifies as a resident under the substantial presence test. Some exceptions may allow the foreigner to establish a termination date within the calendar year, rather than at the end.

A foreigner is deemed income tax resident in the U.S. in any year in which the individual is physically present in the U.S. for 183 days or more. This is the important number of days spent in the U.S. for income tax residency: 183 days.

However, another way the 183 days test may be satisfied can be an unpleasant surprise for many.

The 121 day rule many foreigners do not know about. Foreigners who visit the U.S. to stay with their family or use a vacation home may be visiting too many days each year!

If a foreigner is physically present in the U.S. more than 30 days in a calendar year, it is necessary to determine whether the foreigner has been physically present for at least 183 days over the three-year period ending on the last day of the current year using a weighted average.

So first find the first year a foreigner is physically present in the U.S. more than 30 days. Starting with that year, as long as the foreigner was not in the U.S. more than 121 days that year and for each of the next two years, then there is no income tax residency.

The test works this way:

Days in the present year are multiplied by 1;

Days in the previous year are multiplied by 1/3;

Days in the next immediate preceding year are multiplied by 1/6.

As an example: Say an individual was in the U.S. for more then 30 days in 2013. Actual days are 120 days in 2013, 2014 and 2015. This is on the average spending four months a year in the U.S. at a second home.

2013   120 days x 1 = 120

2014   120 days x 1/3 = 40

2015   120 days x 1/6 = 20

Total: = 180 days

No income tax residency.

But, what happens if the same foreigner visited for 122 days for each of those years?

2013   122 days x 1 = 122

2014   122 days x 1/3 = 40.6667

2015   122 days x 1/6 = 20.3333

Total: = 183 days

Income tax residency has been established in the U.S. Many foreigners who buy a second home in the U.S. spend just a few too many days not realizing they have become U.S. income tax residents!

This example illustrates an important point. An individual is deemed present in the U.S. for a day if any time is spent in the U.S. during that day. This is a potential trap for the unwary!

The exceptions to this automatic presence in a day are the following foreign persons who are considered exempt:

* Commuters to Mexico and/from Canada;

* Travelers spending days in transit between two foreign points;

* Persons with medical conditions that prevent departure;

* Foreign government official on an A or G visa;

* Teachers or trainees in the United States on a J or Q visa, and not physically present more than two calendar years out of the last six calendar years in the U.S.

However, if the foreign teacher's compensation during the six year period is paid by a foreign employer, the two year exemption period is extended to four years.

* Students on an F, J, M or Q visa for no more than five calendar years;

and

* Professional athletes competing in a charitable event.

For family members, they may also be exempt. Members of the immediate family who are with an exempt foreigner in the United States are also exempt individuals.

Closer Connection to a Foreign Home Test:

A foreigner who is physically present in the U.S. for less than 183 days, but satisfies the substantial presence test via the more then 121 days test, may escape U.S. income tax residency status if it can be shown that the foreigner has a closer connection to another country and has a tax home in that foreign country. Closer connection to a foreign country can be established by showing that the foreigner has more significant contacts with the foreign country than with the U.S.

A foreigner must file IRS form 8840 to establish and prove this closer connection with a foreign country. Using this exemption from U.S. income tax requires planning. A foreigner should receive competent U.S. tax advice.

2. Foreign Persons Investing in the U.S.

Foreign persons are taxed on sources of income from the United States. This may be either income which is considered to be effectively connected income to a U.S. trade or business (See discussion in 3. below) or income from passive income sources in the U.S. A few types of passive source income are exempt from U.S. income tax. A tax treaty between the U.S. and a foreign country may also lower the tax rate or exempt certain types of income from U.S. income taxes.

Foreigners are not taxed on interest income earned on U.S. bank accounts and on most capital gains. Real estate does not qualify for the tax exempt capital gain treatment. The Internal Revenue Code Section 897, "FIRPTA", the Foreign Investment in Real Property Tax Act, treats the gain by a foreigner on the disposition of an interest in United States real property as effectively connected business income subject to regular federal income tax. This means the gain does not receive exempt capital gain tax treatment, but rather is taxed as ordinary income. See detailed discussion on FIRPTA in Part Three.

Because the income tax rules for foreigners are very different from the income tax rules for U.S. taxpayers, it is important to understand how a foreigner may be taxed.

Nonresident foreigners must pay U.S. income taxes on U.S. source passive income at a tax rate of 30% of the gross passive income. Passive income is that income not connected with a U.S. trade or business. This includes such items as dividends, interest, royalties, and rents. There are a few exceptions for capital gains and interest. FDAP (FDAP is an acronym for "fixed or determinable annual or periodical gains, profits, and income.")

Capital gains from the sale of stock or other personal property are not taxable. The sale of real estate is not exempt as a capital gain and is taxed differently. See discussion in Part Three below.

Interest paid to a foreigner outside of the U.S., when paid under a note which has specific language as to how the payments are to be made and to whom, can also avoid this 30% withholding tax. This is the portfolio interest exemption. Rules are becoming more restrictive by the IRS to use this valuable exclusion from the 30%

withholding tax. It is important to find out the rules.

Passive income must automatically be paid to the IRS at year end by the 30% withholding tax. It is based upon the gross amount of income earned with no deductions. There is strict liability for the payment of the withholding tax due to the IRS. Whoever has control over that income is liable if the withholding tax is not paid to the IRS. This means that a property manager, who collects rent on real estate for a foreigner out of the country, has the liability to make sure the 30% of the gross rent is paid into the IRS each year on time. Otherwise, the property manger can be held liable by the IRS.

A foreigner can make an election to pay income taxes on passive income and file a U.S. income tax return. With this election, the foreigner is taxed on the net passive income at the graduated tax rates that apply to U.S. taxpayers. Deductions related to the investment property can be taken and often reduce the tax liability to zero. No deductions can be taken by a foreigner on real estate or personal property in the U.S. that is not held for the production of income, such as a vacation home.

If the U.S. has an income tax treaty with the country of residence of the foreigner, the withholding rate on various types of passive income may be lower.

3. Foreign Persons Doing Business in the U.S.

A foreign person or corporation that engages in a continuous or regular business activity in the United States is most likely engaged in a trade or business within the United States. A trade or business does not occur with the ownership of unimproved real property or residential property held for personal use. Further, ownership of a single piece of property rented on a net lease basis (i.e. where the tenant is required to pay all expenses connected with the real estate) is not a U.S. trade or business. When a foreigner, or through its agents, actively manage commercial property and pays all expenses, taxes, and insurance, then there is a U.S. trade or business.

A foreign partner of a partnership or limited liability company (LLC) that is engaged in a U.S. trade or business will also be considered to be engaged in a U.S. trade or business. The opposite result occurs if a foreigner owns shares in a corporation that is engaged in a U.S. trade or business. The foreign shareholder is not considered to be engaged in a U.S. trade or business.

Nonresident foreigners must pay U.S. income taxes on U.S. trade or business income. This income is taxed on net income from the U.S. trade or business at the regular U.S. federal income tax rates which range from 15 % to 39%.

Income taxed as trade or business income requires the filing of a U.S. income tax return to show the income, claim any deductions and calculate the net tax and tax rate.

Gains on the disposition of real property interests are taxed differently. See discussion in Part Three below. The gains from the sale of a U.S. real property interest ("USRPI"), such as real estate, or interests in partnerships, LLCs, trusts, and U.S. corporations that own primarily U.S. real estate, are taxed as trade or business income, whether or not the foreigner is actually engaged in a U.S. trade or business.

If the U.S. has an income tax treaty with the country of residence of the foreigner, the tax rate may be lower.

4. Foreign Companies Investing in the U.S. or Doing Business in the U.S.

A corporation's tax residency is either U.S. (domestic) or foreign. U.S. tax law determines residency of a corporation based on the jurisdiction of formation, but certain other countries determine residency based on where the corporation is managed or controlled. As a result, a corporation could be considered resident in two countries, raising the possibility of double taxation. Many income tax treaties resolve this problem. However, for transactions not covered by treaty, this situation can cause significant double taxation issues.

A foreign company's U.S. taxable income is either: investment income or income that is effectively connected with a trade or business in the United States. As with foreign person discussed above, investment income consists of interest, dividends, certain rents and royalties, and similar types of income from passive investments.

Business income would be taxed at the graduated tax rates for corporations. These rates range from 15% to 35%.

Effectively connected income consists of business income related to U.S. activities. In order to have effectively connected income, a foreign company must first have a U.S. trade or business. Once it is established that a foreign company has a U.S. trade or business, its effectively connected income will consist of all U.S. source business income and certain foreign source income that is associated with the U.S. trade or business.

The U.S. will tax all business profits that are effectively connected to the U.S. trade or business. Even profits earned by a foreign company that has no U.S. office may be taxed. Under most income tax treaties, foreign companies will not be subject to U.S. tax on business profits unless they have a permanent establishment in the United States.

A permanent establishment means in most cases an office or fixed place of business located in the U.S. or the existence of employees or dependent agents that regularly exercise the authority in the United States to conclude contracts on behalf of the company.

PART TWO: TRANSFER TAXES

The U.S. transfer tax system includes the worldwide assets of U.S. citizens and those domiciled in the U.S. All taxable transfers made during life and at death are included and taxed under a single progressive tax rate.

For non-domiciled residents in the U.S., there are some very important planning choices between income tax and estate tax results. As an example, a foreign person may be working in the U.S. or have just received a green card and is now income tax resident. Many foreign countries do not impose an estate or gift tax on persons domiciled in their country. Therefore the same foreign person being taxed for income tax purposes may not want to be deemed to have a domicile here and be subject to the high U.S. estate and gift tax rates.

The U.S. has entered into estate and gift tax treaties with many countries. The U.S. maintains estate, gift, or combined estate and gift treaties with: Australia,

Austria, Belgium, Denmark, Finland, France, Germany, Ireland, Italy, Japan, The Netherlands, Norway, South Africa, Sweden, Switzerland, and the United Kingdom.

There was an estate treaty with Canada, but following Canada's replacement of its estate tax with a capital gains tax, the treaty was terminated in 1985. The U.S.-Canada Income Tax Treaty was amended by Protocol to address the double taxation where both Canada capital gains and U.S. estate tax apply.

GIFT TAXES

1. Gift Tax Rules If Domiciled in the U.S.

A U.S. citizen, or a person domiciled in the U.S., is taxed on gifts of property located anywhere in the world. An exception is gifts made to charities which usually pass free of tax.

An exception is made for gifts of present interests that do not exceed the annual exclusion amount allowed by the IRS each year. As an example, $14,000 in gifts per person in 2014 is the annual exclusion and these are not taxed. This amount is generally increased somewhat each year by the IRS.

Gifts to a U.S. citizen spouse in any amount, which are qualify for the marital deduction, are not taxable. To qualify for the marital deduction, the property gifted must not be a terminable interest. That is, the spouse's interest in the property must not be subject to expiration due to the passage of time, the occurrence of some future event, or the failure of some future event to occur.

If the recipient spouse is not a U.S. citizen, the annual exclusion for 2014 is $145,000 for transfers to a non-U.S. citizen spouse. This amount is generally increased somewhat each year by the IRS.

There also is a unified credit, which can be used to transfer assets during life by gift or a death. This credit allows a person to make lifetime gifts totaling $5,340,000 in 2014 without incurring gift tax (or transfer $5,340,000 at death without estate tax). This amount is generally increased somewhat each year by the IRS. The lifetime gift credit is separate from the annual exclusion of $14,000. If a person makes more than $14,000 in gift in a given year, then he or she needs to file Form 709: United States Gift Tax Return. The gift is reported and the lifetime credit can be used in whole or in part to reduce or eliminate the gift tax due. If the credit is used during lifetime for gifts, then there is less credit left at the time of death to reduce the estate tax.

2. Gift Tax Rules If Not Deemed Domiciled In The U.S.

Gifts made by a non- domiciled foreigner, even if resident in the U.S., are generally not subject to the U.S. gift tax except transfers of tangible property located in the U.S..

Gifts received by U.S. residents (for income tax purposes) in 2014 of more than $100,000 received from non-U.S. residents or $15,358 from foreign entities must be reported on Form 3520, Annual Return To Report transactions With Foreign Trusts and Receipt of Certain Foreign Gifts. The amount allowed for gifts from foreign entities has also generally been increased somewhat each year by the IRS. Failure to report may result in civil penalties of 5% of the amount of the gift for each month the failure to report continues. Such penalties are not to exceed 25% of the total value of the gift. The gifts are not taxable income but must be reported.

Example: Foreign buyers sometimes transfer cash to buy homes for U.S. relatives. These transfers should be documented.

ESTATE TAX

The U.S. federal estate tax is due 9 months after death.

1. Foreigners Domiciled in the U.S.

The estate tax rate is 40% for net asset value over $5,340,000 in 2014. This amount may be increased somewhat by the IRS each year, or could drop to a much lower level in the future if budget proposals are passed. The tax applies to the worldwide assets of every U.S. citizen, or foreigner deemed domiciled in the U.S. The taxable estate is comprised of all property owned worldwide by the decedent, and property transferred during the decedent's life over which some measure of enjoyment or control was maintained, revocable transfers, and transfers of certain property within three years of death, etc. Transfers at death to charities and to a surviving U.S. citizen spouse are generally not taxed. If the transfer is to a non U.S. citizen spouse, a special type of trust can be used to defer estate taxes. This trust is known as a qualified domestic trust (QDOT).

2. Non-Domiciled Foreigners Resident in the U.S. or Green card Holders

U.S. estate tax for foreigners not deemed domiciled in the U.S. is calculated on U.S. assets owned by the deceased foreigner. Only $60,000 in U.S. assets can be owned at death to avoid U.S. estate taxes. All value of U.S. assets over $60,000 is taxable and as high as 40%. This is a very high tax risk for a foreigner owning assets in the U.S. The amount has not been increased for years. Many States in the U.S. also impose their own estate tax. The State estate tax rate can be as high as 19%. These taxes are due nine months after death.

A deceased foreigner's estate may be able to take advantage of a tax treaty between the U.S. and their country of domicile to reduce or eliminate U.S. estate taxes.

A person acquires a domicile by living there, even for a

brief period, if they have no definite intention of leaving. Physical presence in the U.S., without the intent to remain in the U.S. indefinitely, is not sufficient to constitute domicile. The intent to change domicile is not effective unless there is actual departure. Domicile requires not only physical presence, but also intent to remain permanently. This can lead to the individual being considered a resident for U.S. income tax purposes, but a not domiciled for estate or gift tax purposes.

Although an individual's intent is paramount in determining his domicile, the courts and tax authorities can also look at subjective factors in order to determine domicile. Important items are: (a) the location and relative importance of dwellings maintained by the foreigner inside and outside of the U.S., (b) frequency of travel between the U.S. and other countries, (c) the location, value, and size of the foreigner's home(s) and valued personal possessions, (d) the location of the individual's family, friends, important social contacts, and business, (e) the age of any children and the location of their school, and (f) declarations of residence or intent made in visa applications or re-entry permits, wills, gifts, trust instruments, letters, and oral statements.

The duration of an individual's stay in the U.S. will not necessarily be determinative of status as a domiciliary or non-domiciliary, nor will immigration status provide a clear test.

As a planning point, since the ownership of U.S. real estate is an important factor in finding a foreigner as domiciled in the U.S., it is worthwhile to plan how title to real estate should be held.

PROBATE IMPACTS FOREIGNERS OWNING U.S. ASSETS

Probate is an expensive and unnecessary court process to administer property upon a person's death. In every state in the U.S. in which a decedent owned property, there will be a probate. In some states the court process called probate is very expensive. In any case, it is a public record. Family privacy is lost. It is important for a foreign person owning assets in the U.S. to find out about the probate process and how it can be avoided to save time, money and family privacy.

PART THREE: FOREIGN OWNERSHIP OF U.S. REAL ESTATE

For foreigners, individuals or entities, there are specific tax rules which impact the ownership of real estate in the U.S. Below are the general tax considerations for foreign buyers of U.S. real estate.

FOREIGN INVESTMENT IN REAL PROPERTY TAX ACT (FIRPTA)

1. United States Real Property Interest – a USRPI

Foreigners acquiring an interest in real estate in the U.S., either directly or through a U.S. corporation or other U.S. entity, must understand how the rules of FIRPTA will affect them when they dispose of their interest.

FIRPTA treats the gain or loss of a foreign investor or a foreign entity from the disposition of a U.S. real property interest, a USRPI, as income or loss from a U.S. trade or business. That results in ordinary income, not capital gain. It is not possible to avoid U.S. tax on the disposition of real property by holding the property indirectly through a U.S. corporation and selling its stock.

2. United States Real Property Holding Company – a "USRPHC"

A USRPI includes shares and other equity interests in a U.S. corporation that was considered to be a U.S. real property holding company, a "USRPHC", at any time during a five year look back.

A corporation is considered to be a USRPHC if in general the fair market value of its USRPI is 50% or more of the sum of its assets. The test period to determine if a foreigner owns an interest in a USRPHC is the shorter of the time the foreigner has owned the stock or equity interest, or a five year look back period ending on the date of disposition of the stock or equity in the corporation. A foreign entity or foreign investor is not subject to U.S. tax on the disposition of its interest in a U.S. corporation if it is not a USRPHC in the test period.

A USRPI does not include an interest in a publicly traded domestic corporation unless the investor owned more than 5% of the fair market value of such stock at any time during the five year period ending on the date of the investor's disposition of such stock. A REIT (real estate investment trust) also may avoid FIRPTA. An interest in a domestically controlled REIT does not constitute USRPI.

Domestically controlled (less than 50% foreign

ownership by value) REITs are not considered to be USRPIs under FIRPTA. Consequently, foreign investors who hold an interest in domestically controlled REITs will not be subject to tax under FIRPTA upon the sale of their shares. Nevertheless, dividend distributions made by a REIT to foreign investors and attributable to the REIT's gains from sales or exchanges of USRPI are subject to U.S. tax under FIRPTA.

A REIT is a special purpose entity for U.S. federal income purposes. As long as specific terms exist for the ownership, character and mix of assets and income, and distribution rules are met,a REIT is allowed to deduct dividends paid to their shareholders so that their earnings are not subject to corporate-level tax.

The "taint" of USRPHC status can be removed if the corporation disposes of all of its USRPIs in taxable transactions prior to the disposition of its stock. In this situation, U.S. tax on all appreciation in USRPIs will have been paid and there is no longer a need to capture that appreciation in the stock value. When property is sold and tax is paid at the U.S. corporation level, then the shares are no longer subject to FIRPTA. The U.S. corporation can then be liquidated for tax free capital gain treatment.

3. Withholding Tax Required

When a foreigner disposes of a U.S. real property interest, the buyer must withhold taxes equal to 10% of the gross amount of the transaction. There are special withholding rules that apply to distributions and dispositions by corporations, partnerships, trusts, or estates. Usually the withholding is done by the title company handling the sale or transfer. The title company deducts 10% from the gross sales price and sends it to the IRS within 20 days after the closing and transfer of title.

It is possible to avoid this 10% withholding and payment to the IRS if the foreigner requests a FIRPTA clearance certificate from the IRS before the closing and transfer of title. This is done on IRS form 8288 and when the foreigner can prove by documentation to the IRS that the 10% of gross is more tax then the actual tax due on the transfer. The title company will collect the 10% due to the IRS and hold it until the IRS issues the clearance certificate, which can take up to 90 days.

If the buyer fails to withhold the correct tax amount, the purchaser has liability for entire amount of the tax, plus interest and penalties. Therefore, it is very important that the purchaser of U.S. real property determine whether there is a withholding obligation.

There are exceptions to the withholding requirement. These are: 1) The seller may provide the buyer with an affidavit affirming its status as non-foreign; 2) The seller may provide the buyer and the IRS with an affidavit stating that the corporation the stock of which is being transferred is not a USRPHC; 3) The seller may provide the buyer an affidavit stating that the transfer is pursuant to a non-recognition event under the Internal Revenue Code; 4) A non-publicly traded U.S. corporation may furnish an affidavit to the buyer (or alternatively to the seller, who then gives it to the buyer) that its stock is not a USRPI either because it has not been a USRPHC during the relevant period or it has cleansed its taint; 5) The shares in publicly traded corporation are not owned by the seller's more than 5%; or 6) The USRPI is acquired by an individual buyer to be used for residential purposes, as long as the amount realized does not exceed USD 300,000.

4. Exempt from FIRPTA

Stock in a Foreign Corporation is Not Subject to FIRPTA

Only a U.S. corporation can be a USRPHC. The disposition of stock in a foreign corporation can never constitute the disposition of a USRPI.

The gain from the sale of an interest in a foreign corporation is not subject to tax under FIRPTA. Thus, a foreign person may own U.S. real property indirectly through a foreign corporation and ultimately sell the shares of that foreign corporation and avoid U.S. tax on the gain from the sale. Of course, if the foreign corporation holding the USRPI disposes of the USRPI directly, the gain from the sale will be subject to tax under FIRPTA.

An interest in real estate that is held as a creditor is also not subject to FIRPTA. Such interest may include a right of foreclosure on real property under a mortgage, a financing statement, or other instrument securing a debt. A right to share in the appreciation in value of real property or in the gross or net proceeds or profits generated by real property is a USRPI.

TAXATION OF U.S. REAL ESTATE OWNED BY A FOREIGNER

1. Acquisition by a Foreigner Directly on Title

The purchase of real property has no immediate consequences to the foreign buyer. That is why so often a foreigner buys real estate and does not take title in the most tax efficient manner. Title companies cannot give legal or tax advice and can only list the various choices of how to take title: joint tenants, tenants in common, community property, as an unmarried person, etc. Several tax issues associated with the purchase of real estate by a foreign person deserve attention.

a) FIRPTA withholding. Like any buyer, the foreign buyer is a withholding agent for purposes of the 1980 Foreign Investment in Real Property Tax Act (FIRPTA) and must therefore either obtain a certification of non-foreign status from the seller or withhold 10 %of the purchase price (or some lesser amount if the seller produces a withholding certificate from the IRS).

It is very important for the foreign buyer to have the certificate of non-foreign status. When the foreigner later sells the real estate, if they wish to obtain a certificate from the IRS to reduce or avoid the title company withholding 10% of their gross sales price, the foreigner must have that certificate of non-foreign status from the seller they bought the property from.

b) Financing. Not infrequently, foreign buyers pay all cash or at least they don't obtain a mortgage loan at the time of the purchase. If the purchase is financed by a foreign entity, then the interest earned/paid is subject to a 30% withholding tax unless the promissory note/debt is written to eliminate this requirement. A lower treaty rate between countries may lower the 30% required withholding rate. The best financing structure is to have the debt/promissory note written to satisfy IRS requirements which exempt the interest from any withholding tax. This is known as the portfolio interest exception. Basically, it requires the note to contain certain language and for all interest to be paid outside of the U.S. There are restrictions on related party loans.

c) Deductions. Nonresident foreigners are not entitled to itemized deductions (e.g., mortgage interest and property taxes). However, if the acquisition is structured through a corporation, discussed below, expenses related to maintaining the property may be allowed, but personal use of the property may involve actual or imputed rental issues.

d) Imputed rental income. When the home is owned directly by a foreign person, there is no income tax consequence to its occupation by the owner, or income tax or gift tax consequences when property is used by relatives. However, when the home is owned by an entity, the possibility that imputed rental should be charged arises. In the case of a home owned by a corporation, personal use by a shareholder or officer is may cause imputed rental income for the corporation if actual rent is not paid at a fair market rate, and possible gift tax issues for the shareholder or officer.

e) Tax compliance. As long as a home produces no income, there is no need for a nonresident foreigner to file a tax return except for the year of sale. The deductions (mortgage interest, property taxes, and so on) associated with a home held by an individual for personal or family use are not available to the nonresident foreigner.

2. Acquisition through a U.S. corporation

A foreign investor may decide to own U.S. real estate in a U.S. corporation formed to hold title to the property. When a U.S. corporation holds real estate, the taxation of the corporation and the earnings from the real estate must be considered. Also, any gain from the disposition of stock in a U.S. corporation that holds U.S. real estate is subject to U.S. income taxes as ordinary business income, and not exempt as a capital gain on the sale of U.S. stock.

U.S. corporations are taxed as a C corporation, ie., a regular corporation, and pay income tax on their worldwide income. A C corporation is not allowed a deduction for dividends paid to its shareholders. In 2014, the top corporate U.S. tax rate is 35%. Unlike the capital gains tax rates for individuals, there is no lower preferential tax rate for capital gains earned by a C corporation. Thus, a C corporation selling appreciated real estate is taxable on its gain as ordinary income.

A C corporation is taxed differently from an S corporation. An S corporation is formed as a regular corporation, but makes a tax election to be taxed as an S corporation. This means the corporation itself is not taxed. The shareholders are taxed as income and losses pass through to them. An election to be taxed as an S corporation cannot be made if there are any foreign shareholders.

Further tax limitations may also exist on the benefits of holding U.S. real estate through a U.S. corporation. These include the alternative minimum tax and a limitation on interest deductions. Both are complicated and beyond the basic scope of this material.

After the U.S. corporation has earned income and paid its taxes, the question then remains how the foreign investor gets his or her investment back from the U.S. corporation. The foreign investor might be paid a dividend from the after tax earnings of the corporation. Dividends paid are not deductable by a corporation. While dividends generally are subject to the 30% withholding tax for passive income paid to a foreigner, most tax treaties reduce that rate of the withholding tax on dividends. This presumes that the foreigner resides in a country that has an income tax treaty with the U.S.

It may be possible for the foreigner to be paid interest on loans made to the corporation as its shareholder. This gives the corporation an interest deduction for the amounts paid, unlike the dividend where there is no deduction. Interest paid to a foreigner is also subject to the 30% withholding tax for passive income, but as with dividends, most treaties reduce the withholding tax required on interest payments. Again, this presumes that the foreign investor resides in a country that has an income tax treaty with the U.S., and the deduction of the interest is not disallowed. Interest paid may also be exempt from any withholding taxes due to the IRS under the portfolio interest exemption. This is a very valuable tool for structuring loans with unrelated parties.

Another alternative to paying the earnings to the foreign investor is receiving proceeds from the disposition of the corporation's stock. If the corporation is a U.S. Real Property Holding Corporation ("USRPHC"), or was a USRPHC during a five period looking back, the gain resulting from the sale of stock is taxed as ordinary business income and not tax exempt capital gain.

If the U.S. corporation has never been a USRPHC, U.S. taxation may be avoided altogether when the stock is sold and the foreigner has no other contacts in the United States. Earnings may also be repatriated by selling off the assets and liquidating the corporation. If a corporation that is a USRPHC disposes of all its property in a taxable transaction in which the full amount of gain is recognized, the stock in the corporation ceases immediately to be a USRPI, and gain realized by foreign shareholders on the stock qualifies for capital gain. Many income tax treaties exclude from any tax capital gain.

3. Acquisition Through a Foreign Corporation

Foreign corporations owning U.S. real estate are generally taxed on a 30% withholding tax basis on their passive income, and on a net basis, under rules similar to U.S. corporations, on their ordinary business income. Foreign corporations are also subject to an additional tax on U.S. earnings and profits that are not reinvested in their U.S. trade or business. If this added tax applies, the foreign corporation year may be subject to a U.S. tax rate of greater than 50%.

For the foreign shareholder, the after tax earnings of the foreign corporation may be paid back as a dividend. Dividends paid by the foreign corporation generally are not subject to further U.S. taxation. Any interest paid back to the foreign investor by the foreign corporation from its U.S. trade or business in real estate is taxable as U.S. source income, and subject to the 30% withholding tax. An exception may apply for a debt created under the portfolio interest exemption. This exemption has been denied in recent years for transactions between related parties.

The foreign investor shareholder can sell his or her stock in the foreign corporation free of U.S. tax. If the foreign investor creates a foreign corporation, and it owns the stock of the U.S. corporation that owns U.S. real estate, then the foreigner can sell the stock in the foreign corporation and that is not subject to U.S. taxation. The stock does not constitute a USRPI under FIRPTA.

Many foreign investors acquire U.S. real estate through a foreign corporation to avoid U.S. estate tax. However, the foreign corporation ownership may cause problems if the foreign corporation is a partner in a partnership or LLC owning U.S. real estate (see below).

4. Acquisition Through a U.S. Partnership or LLC

Foreign ownership of U.S. real estate through a partnership, or an LLC which is taxed as a partnership, creates separate U.S. tax problems.

A partnership, or an LLC taxed as a partnership because it has more then one member, is not a separate taxpayer. Its income and loss passes through to its partners/members. The partners/members are taxed directly on their share of the partnership's income annually, regardless of whether the income is actually distributed. Each foreign partner of a U.S. partnership must, therefore, file a U.S. income tax return. The normal tax rates applicable to U.S. individuals and corporations apply.

Each partner's tax liability is determined by his or her personal status. Different tax treaties might apply, depending on the residence of the partners.

There are strict withholding tax obligations drafted to make sure that tax is collected quarterly for each foreign partner's share of the partnership's trade or business income. This is required for any foreign partner, regardless if they are an individual or a corporation. A partnership must withhold from a foreign partner's share of the net business income of the partnership each quarter. This is basically requires the partnership to make estimated tax payments on behalf of its foreign partners each quarter. This can severely impact the cash flow of the partnership! Any over-withholding of the foreign partner's regular tax liability is recovered only by the partner through the filing of his or her own tax return at year end. This forced distribution of the estimated tax due the IRS is treated as a distribution out to the foreign partner. This can leave other non-foreign partners at a disadvantage if they too do not receive a distribution each quarter.

When the foreign partner sells his or her partnership interest, the gain from the sale is treated as business income and subject to U.S. tax to the extent it is from the partnership's ownership of U.S. real property. If a partnership sells all of its assets and liquidates, the partners are taxable on their pro rata share of the partnership's gain at their tax rates. If the partnership holds U.S. real estate and has foreign partners, the partnership must pay the IRS the FIRPTA 10% of gross.

PART FOUR: PRE-IMMIGRATION PLANNING.

1. Tax Treaties

The United States has income tax treaties with many countries that encourage foreign investment and prevent the double taxation of income from transactions. The benefits of a treaty apply only to residents of the contracting countries. Most tax treaties provide that income from real property, including income from the direct use of the real property by the owner and the rental income for use of the property, is taxable in the country in which the property is located. Under most U.S. treaties, residents of the treaty country are exempt from U. S. tax on gain from the sale of assets, such as stock, unless such assets form part of the resident's U.S. business, or the assets are U.S. real property. Not all countries tax trusts and limited liability companies the same way as the U.S., so that must be reviewed.

2. Non-Domiciled Status

For individuals immigrating to the U.S., it is a good time to make family gifts either outright or in various forms of entities, such as foreign trusts, foreign foundations, foreign corporate entities and the like. This is because the individual, before he or she becomes subject to the U.S. tax net, can take advantage of the opportunity to move large amounts of net worth out of their name without any incidents of U.S. taxation. This eliminates the need to worry about the estate after U.S. domiciliary status is acquired.

As an example, if a foreigner owns assets that they wish to pass to their children or grandchildren, such as a family business located outside of the U.S., then it is better to make those transfers before the foreign parents become domiciled in the U.S.. Shares in a family company located abroad can be gifted in trust for the children and grandchildren; or the class of shares can be reissued to provide for voting and non-voting rights such that the parents retain control and a preferred share of profits, all before entering the U.S. tax system and its restrictions. Succession planning is best done before U.S. domiciliary status is acquired. The gift tax laws of the foreigners home country must be reviewed and complied with at all times. Many countries do not have a gift tax or have a very limited gift tax. That is the advantage in the pre-immigration tax planning.

3. Foreign Trusts (Drop Off Trust)

A foreign trust is any trust other than a domestic trust, which is a trust where a U.S. court has primary supervision (court test) and at least one U.S. person has the ability to control all substantial decisions of the trust (control test).

If a foreign trust is established before a person becomes tax resident in the U.S., but within 5 years thereafter the person establishes U.S. residency, then on the date of U.S. residency, the assets in the foreign trust will be deemed transferred to the trust for U.S. tax reporting purposes. Planning for pre-immigration would require that the trust be created before that 5 year period.

PART FIVE: REPORTING REQUIREMENTS TO THE IRS, FATCA AND WORLDWIDE REPORTING WITH TIEAS

In 2014 the FATCA (foreign account tax compliance act) became effective for all persons and entities required to report for U.S. income tax purposes. This Act requires a U.S. taxpayer, whether living in the U.S. or abroad, to report foreign owned assets worldwide. The basic threshold is $50,000 of foreign owned assets per taxpayer. Strict penalties apply for failure to report assets under this information return. Foreign governments or financial institutions are required to report account information for U.S. taxpayers to the IRS. Form 8966 is the form required.

The FATCA is extensive and overlaps with other reporting forms required by the IRS. The FATCA reaches further and requires the reporting of assets that previously had not been under a reporting requirement, such as life insurance and annuities.

In addition to the FATCA, there are other reporting obligations.

There has been for many years the requirement to report foreign bank accounts or brokerage accounts over which a U.S. taxpayer has signing authority or can exert control. The maximum amount that can be held in all foreign bank and brokerage accounts together is $10,000. The accounts must be reported on the U.S. income tax return of the taxpayer and a separate form known as the FBAR must be filed. The FBAR is filed separately from the income tax return and cannot be put on an extension. It is due in June of each year. Strict penalties apply for failure to report foreign bank or brokerage accounts. The penalties can be criminal and civil. There are voluntary disclosure programs offered by the IRS which reduce civil penalties and eliminate criminal charges if the taxpayer comes forward before the IRS discovers the accounts. More and more foreign countries are reporting information to the U.S. and the IRS under taxpayer information exchange agreements (TIEAS). Therefore, it is important for a foreigner who has acquired U.S. income tax reporting status to report all foreign owned assets to avoid penalties.

Other information returns which are required are Form 3520 and Form 3520A, the creation of a foreign trust or the beneficial interest in a foreign trust; Form 5471, the ownership of 10% or more of the ownership or value of a foreign corporation; and Form 5472, the ownership of a 25% or more interest in a U.S. corporation by a foreigner.

A foreigner may be both a nonresident alien and a resident alien during the same tax year. This usually occurs in the year you arrive in or depart from the United States. If a foreigner is U.S. resident for the calendar year, but was not a U.S. resident at any time during the preceding calendar year, then the foreigner is a U.S. resident only for the part of the calendar year that begins on the residency starting date, and nonresident alien for the part of the year before that date.

A special rule applies for those with green cards. If the

foreigner meets the green card test at any time during a calendar year, but did not meet the substantial presence test for that year, the residency starting date is the first day in the calendar year on which the foreigner is present in the United States as a lawful permanent resident. If both the substantial presence test and the green card test are met, then residency starts on the date that is the earlier of the first day during the year the foreigner is present in the United States under the substantial presence test or as a lawful permanent resident.

Many foreigners who acquire U.S. taxpayer status though residency or a green card are shocked to discover that they must report worldwide assets and pay income tax on the income or earnings from those assets. This applies whether income or earnings are distributed from the foreign entity or account to the foreigner in the U.S.

It is very important for foreigners thinking of acquiring U.S. residency or a green card to get important tax information on their obligations before they acquire U.S. tax payer status. If residency or green card status has already been acquired, it is still important to get the information and be able to file correctly. There may be opportunities for tax planning if done in time and they foreigner should find out about the choices that can be made. Sometimes it may involve giving up a green card or residency to get the best tax result. A green card holder for eight years cannot give up a green card without it being considered expatriation. If the person's net worth is 2 million or more, then the IRS will tax the expatriating foreigner on their worldwide assets as if they are sold the day the green card is surrendered. This is an example of why a foreigner must understand the U.S. tax rules that apply in time to make the best choices for themselves and their family.

Goodbye

About the Author

Mary Vigal, J.D., LL.M. (Tax)

Is a U.S. tax lawyer and consultant, practicing over 35 years. She is a tax specialist certified by The State Bar of California Board of Legal Specialization since 1979. One of her areas of expertise is advising foreign persons or businesses on the basic tax implications of residing or investing in the U.S. She is licensed by the Dept of Licensing of Washington State as a Real Estate Instructor in the area of Taxation.

 Ms. Vigal is a former full time associate professor of law at the Graduate School of Taxation of Golden Gate University in San Francisco California, a visiting professor in taxation at the Santa Clara University School of Law in Santa Clara California, and a former lecturer at the San Jose State Graduate School of Business in San Jose California.

 Ms. Vigal received her B.A. degree in Economics from the Colorado College, her J.D. degree from the University of Santa Clara and her LL.M. (tax) degree, from Golden Gate University.

Mary offers tax consultations and can be reached for questions or to arrange a personal consultation, by e mail: Mary at mary@condado-group.com

Disclaimer

This booklet is intended to be an introduction to the U.S. tax system as it applies to foreigners. It is not a substitute for personalized advice from a professional advisor. The information is current; but tax laws change almost daily. No guarantee can be made as to the accuracy of the information contained within. Purchasing the booklet does not create any client relationship or other advisory, fiduciary, or professional services relationship with the publisher or with the author.

The booklet includes information about taxation. While nothing contained within should be construed as personalized tax advice, any tax information is not intended or written to be used, and cannot be used, for the purpose of avoiding penalties under the Internal Revenue Code or promoting, marketing, or recommending to another party any transaction or matter addressed in this booklet.

www.ingramcontent.com/pod-product-compliance
Lightning Source LLC
Chambersburg PA
CBHW040815200526
45159CB00024B/2981